HARRY POTTER

THE AMAZING QUIZ BOOK

Frankie Taylor

Andrews UK Limited

First published worldwide in 2013 by
Andrews UK Limited
The Hat Factory
Bute Street
Luton, LU1 2EY
www.andrewsuk.com

The Quiz

The Questions

Quidditch

1. How many people are there on a standard Quidditch team? **7**

2. How many points is a goal worth? **10**

3. And how many for catching the Snitch? **150**

4. True or false: the Quidditch World Cup happens every five years? **False**

5. How many Quidditch fouls are listed in the rules?

6. When was the last time that all of them were committed in one match?

7. Name any of the Quidditch teams from the continent of Africa. ~~_____~~

8. Which team does Oliver Wood play for after graduating from Hogwarts?

9. Which two teams contest the world cup final that Harry watches? **Bulgairia Romainia**

10. Who is the author of the book 'Quidditch through the Ages'?

Spells (Easy) - Part 1

What do these spells do?

11. Reparo

12. Accio

13. Engorgio

14. Expelliarmus

15. Riddikulus

16. Incendio

17. Lumos

18. Sonorus

19. Confundo

20. Muffliato

Who Plays (Easy)

In the films, who plays these characters?

21. Harry Potter *Daniel*
22. Rubeus Hagrid
23. Uncle Vernon Dursley
24. Ginny Weasley
25. Ron Weasley *Rupet*
26. Hermione Granger *Emma Watson*
27. Draco Malfoy
28. Nearly Headless Nick
29. Severus Snape ~~Rick~~ *Alan rickman*
30. Sirius Black

Gryffindors

31. Which Gryffindor girl did Ron date for a short time, once receiving a *My Sweetheart* necklace from her?

32. What was the Creevey's father's occupation?

33. What position does Fay Dunbar play at Quidditch?

34. What form does Seamus's Patronus take?

35. Who does Angelina Johnson attend the Yule ball with?

36. What is Neville's toad called?

37. Why could Cormac McLaggen not take part in Quidditch trials in his sixth year?

38. Who gives Harry a love-potion-laced box of Chocolate Cauldrons?

39. Which Gryffindor student hosts Potterwatch?

40. What was in the note from Professor Snape that Demelza Robbins brought to Harry?

Harry Potter (Easy)

41. Where can you find Harry's thunderbolt scar?

42. What were Harry's parents called?

43. Into which other house did the sorting hat consider putting Harry?

44. What is Harry's middle name?

45. Which birthday was Harry (not) celebrating when he found out he was a Wizard?

46. Harry was the only known survivor of which curse?

47. What was Harry's first broomstick whilst at Hogwarts?

48. Name Harry's muggle aunt and uncle?

49. Who does Harry eventually marry at the end of the series?

50. The Dursleys always had always led Harry to believe that his parents had died in which way?

Hermione Granger (Easy)

51. What is Hermione's middle name?

52. What do her parents do?

53. Which house is Hermione sorted into?

54. Where did Hermione first meet Harry?

55. Which creature once petrified Hermione?

56. Who does Hermione eventually marry?

57. Name the object that allowed Hermione to attend more classes than the other students thought possible.

58. With whom did Hermione attend the Yule Ball?

59. After which year did Hermione leave Hogwarts?

60. What is the name of Hermione's pet cat?

Hogwarts Staff (Easy)

61. Name Filch's cat.

62. Which centaur becomes Hogwarts divination teacher?

63. What does madame Pomfrey use to heal Harry's arm after Gilderoy Lockhart has made a real mess of it?

64. What is the full name of the professor who has Voldemort's head under his turban?

65. Who is the astronomy teacher at Hogwarts during Harry's time there?

66. Name one of Snape's nicknames.

67. Which house is Professor Sprout head of?

68. Who sacked Professor Trelawney?

69. What was the name of the muggle studies teacher who was killed by Voldemort?

70. Who took over from Hagrid as the teacher for care of magical creatures?

Magical Creatures (Easy)

Can you name the creature being described?

71. A species of giant spider native to the rainforests of Southeastern Asia.

72. Has the head and torso of a human on the lower body of a horse.

73. Often referred to as the 'biting fairy', venom used for skiving snackboxes.

74. Toothless brown worm that eats cabbage and lettuce.

75. Has the front legs, wings and head of a giant eagle, and the hindquarters of a horse.

76. Magical feline similar to a large housecat.

77. Mischievous magical prankster native to Ireland.

78. Infests mistletoe - according to Luna Lovegood.

79. Large scarlet-coloured bird which can be reborn from its ashes.

80. Skeletal horse only visible to those who have witnessed death.

Sirius Black

81. What is Sirius's nickname?

82. How many years did he spend in Azkaban?

83. Who eventually killed Sirius?

84. ...and what relationship were they to him?

85. How did Sirius escape from Azkaban?

86. What did Sirius give to Hagrid at the time of James and Lily Potter's death?

87. What is the address of the house that Sirius bequeaths to Harry?

88. And who is the house elf who lives there?

89. What was the name of Sirius's younger brother?

90. What nickname do Harry, Ron and Hermione give to Sirius so they can talk about him in public?

Spells (Easy) - Part 2

What would you say if you wanted to cast the following spells?

91. The Killing Curse.

92. This opens or unlocks doors.

93. Turns an object into a portkey.

94. Silences the target immediately.

95. Conjures a Patronus.

96. Inflicts unbearable pain on the target.

97. Renders the victim unconscious.

98. Reveals the last spell cast by a wand.

99. Removes memories of an event from the target.

100. Conjures the dark mark.

The Weasleys (Easy)

101. What is Ron's full name?

102. What does Ron's boggart transform into?

103. Name all of Ron's brothers and sisters.

104. In the final story, one of the twins loses his life during the battle at Hogwarts - but which twin is it?

105. Who or what is Errol?

106. Ginny took possession of a diary which forced her to open something that endangered the life of many students. What did she open?

107. What is the (animal) name of Ron's pet rat?

108. Charlie Weasley graduated from Hogwarts and studied dragons in which country?

109. During the battle at the astronomy tower, Bill was attacked by which creature?

110. What is make of the car which Ron flies Harry to Hogwarts in one year?

Dumbledore and Family (Easy)

111. What is the name of Dumbledore's phoenix?

112. Which house did the sorting hat place Albus Dumbledore in during his time as a student at Hogwarts?

113. One reason for Dumbledore's fame is due to his discovery of the twelve uses for what?

114. What position was Dumbledore repeatedly offered but never accepted?

115. On one fateful day in June, Dumbledore is pushed from the astronomy tower by whom?

116. What are the names of Dumbledore's brother and sister?

117. Which member of Dumbledore's family was placed in Azkaban for attacking Muggles?

118. Aberforth Dumbledore was the owner of which pub located in Hogsmeade?

119. What colour was Dumbledore's beard as a young wizard?

120. What does Dumbledore use to 'play back' his memories?

The Malfoys (Easy)

121. Name Draco Malfoy's two sidekicks.

122. Malfoy was put on detention with Hagrid for being out past curfew. He referred to his punishment as 'servant's stuff', but what were they looking for?

123. When Draco is assigned to kill Dumbledore, he becomes stressed leading him to confide in which mudblood?

124. Draco witnessed the murder of which Hogwarts teacher?

125. What core does Draco's wand have?

126. What are Draco Malfoy's parents called?

127. True or False: the Malfoy's are supposedly a family of purebloods.

128. Before Narcissa's marriage to Lucius Malfoy, what was her surname?

129. Which animal attacks Malfoy causing him to 'nearly lose his arm'?

130. Which animal is Draco turned into by the 'fake' Professor Moody?

Who Plays (Medium) - Part 1

In the films, who plays these characters?

131. Professor Minerva McGonagall

132. Professor Quirinus Quirrell

133. Molly Weasley

134. Fred & George Weasley

135. Neville Longbottom

136. Vincent Crabbe

137. Gregory Goyle

138. Madame Hooch

139. Lucius Malfoy

140. Professor Gilderoy Lockhart

Slytherins

141. How did the Bloody Baron die?

142. With which Slytherin student does Hermione physically fight in duelling club?

143. What positions do Crabbe and Goyle play in Quidditch?

144. What spell does Crabbe cast which leads to his - and Goyle's death?

145. For how many years did Marcus Flint study at Hogwarts?

146. During their first flying lesson, who teases Parvati Patil for defending Neville when his Remembrall is stolen by Malfoy?

147. During Slughorn's lunch on the Hogwarts Express, which Slytherin student tells of how his mother was left pots of galleons from her many husbands, all of whom died suspicious deaths?

148. Apart from Harry and Neville, who else can see the thestrals during Hagrid's class?

149. Who was captain of the Slytherin Quidditch team from Harry's third year onwards?

150. Who is Slytherin's seeker before Draco Malfoy is given the job?

Harry Potter (Medium)

151. On which date is Harry's birthday?

152. How old (in years and months) was Harry when Voldemort tried to murder him?

153. During a tea leaf reading in divination, what shape appeared in the bottom of Harry's cup?

154. Who first shows Harry the diary of Tom Riddle?

155. When Harry let the boa constrictor out during his trip to the zoo, where did it plan on going?

156. When Harry first met Oliver Wood on the Quidditch pitch, he compared the game to which muggle sport?

157. Name the school that Harry was instructed to tell aunt Marge he attended.

158. Which type of dragon was Harry pitted against in his tri-wizard task?

159. Harry and Voldemort's wands share the same core; what is it?

160. What did Dumbledore leave to Harry in his will?

Patronuses

Can you name the animal form of the Patronus of these characters?

161. Harry Potter

162. Ron Weasley

163. Ginny Weasley

164. Albus Dumbledore

165. Kingsley Shacklebolt

166. Luna Lovegood

167. Severus Snape

168. Dolores Umbridge

169. Cho Chang

170. Aberforth Dumbledore

Hermione Granger
(Medium)

171. When Harry and Ron first met Hermione, they didn't seem to like her - she came across as a know-it-all. What single act however changed their perspective of her?

172. What is the full name of the society Hermione founded which concerns itself with rights for House elves?

173. The treatment of which house elf - and by whom - caused her to set it up?

174. What is the name of Hermione's two children at the end of the series?

175. Which other house did the sorting hat consider putting Hermione in?

176. ...and why?

177. Whose hair did Hermione think she had which actually turned out to be their cat's?

178. What form does Hermione's Patronus take?

179. What was Hermione left in Dumbledore's will?

180. What is the name of the charm that Hermione uses to enchant the coins for Dumbledore's Army?

Anagrams (Medium)

These are the names of Harry Potter characters, but the letters are jumbled up. Can you unscramble them?

181. Trophy Rater

182. Slick Airbus

183. Fly Cod Aroma

184. Go Valued Loon

185. A Bulbous Meddler

186. Nose Lawyer

187. Amusing Fannies

188. Enrage Grim Heron

189. Bushier Guard

190. Melon Bottle Loving

Lord Voldemort

191. What was Tom Riddle's middle name?

192. What is the name given to Voldemort's inner circle of Followers?

193. What is the name of Voldemort's pet snake?

194. What was the name of the orphanage Tom grew up in?

195. In which village did Tom's father live?

196. What type of wood is the wand that Voldemort takes off Lucius Malfoy in order to kill Harry made of?

197. What was Tom's mother's maiden name?

198. After graduating from Hogwarts, Tom worked where for a short amount of time?

199. What are the names of the two children Tom took into a cave during his time at the orphanage?

200. Recite the verse Peter Pettigrew chants to 'resurrect' Voldemort in Godric's Hollow.

Spells (Medium)

For the first five questions, what do these spells do?

For the second five, what would you say if you wanted to cast them?

201. Aguamenti

202. Incarcerous

203. Glisseo

204. Tarantallegra

205. Diffindo

206. Causes birds to attack a target.

207. Reveals nearby humans.

208. Causes the target's teeth to grow at an alarming rate.

209. The target feels like they're being tickled.

210. Makes things lower.

Ravenclaws

211. Which girl did Cedric invite to the Yule Ball before Harry could pluck up the courage?

212. Which Ravenclaw student during Harry's time at Hogwarts had an uncle by the name of Damocles?

213. What potion does Eddie Carmichael claim helped him achieve nine 'outstandings' in his O.W.L. exams?

214. Name Percy Weasley's Ravenclaw girlfriend from his Hogwarts years.

215. Name the ghost who haunts the first-floor girls' bathroom.

216. Parvati Patil is sorted into Gryffindor, but who is her twin who is placed into Ravenclaw?

217. Helena Ravenclaw is Ravenclaw's house ghost - but what is she better known as?

218. When Harry first attends Hogwarts, which teacher is head of Ravenclaw house?

219. Which Ravenclaw student was Fleur Delacour's date at the Yule Ball?

220. Apart from Harry, who dates both Ginny Weasley and Cho Chang?

Hogwarts Staff (Medium)

221. Where was Professor Binns when he died?

222. Which teacher conducts the school choir?

223. What is Madam Hooch's first name?

224. Who does Hagrid replace as the teacher for care of magical creatures?

225. What is Gilderoy Lockhart's favourite colour?

226. What creature was in the paddling pool Professor Lupin used for the third year students' end-of-year obstacle course test?

227. Name the spell Professor McGonagall uses to animate the warriors of Hogwarts.

228. Which village is Professor Slughorn hiding in when Dumbledore and Harry find him?

229. What law did Umbridge once propose about Merpeople?

230. Who was the caretaker at Hogwarts when Mr and Mrs Weasley attended?

Dobby

231. Which family did Dobby serve before being freed?

232. What unusual punishment did Dobby once inflict on his hands?

233. How much was Dobby paid per week for working in the kitchens at Hogwarts?

234. When Dobby rescues his friends from Malfoy Manor, under whose orders is he working?

235. Where is Dobby's grave?

236. Which Quidditch ball does Dobby enchant during a match?

237. Name the female elf who Dobby looks after when she is freed.

238. How did Dobby come across the room of requirement?

239. What does Dobby name Ron?

240. What are Dobby's final words?

Who Plays (Medium) - Part 2

In the films, who plays these characters?

241. Colin Creevey

242. Arthur Weasley

243. Professor Sybil Trelawney

244. Peter Pettigrew

245. Barty Crouch Junior

246. Cedric Diggory

247. Cho Chang

248. Fleur Delacour

249. Lord Voldemort

250. Rufus Scrimgeour

Hermione Granger (Hard)

251. Name two of the four girls Hermione shares a dormitory with.

252. In The Philosopher's (or Sorcerer's) stone, what spell does Hermione conjure to free the trio from the Devil's Snare?

253. What did Hermione transfigure a match into during her first class with Professor McGonagall?

254. Name one of the two things Hermione smells in the Love Potion.

255. With whom does Hermione attend Professor Slughorn's Christmas party?

256. What method of flying did Hermione use in the battle of the seven Potters?

257. ...and who accompanied her?

258. Hermione used polyjuice potion to infiltrate the Ministry of Magic - but who does she turn into?

259. What magical plant does Hermione use to heal Harry's bite from Nagini?

260. Describe Hermione's wand.

Magical Creatures (Hard)

Can you name the creature being described?

261. A cross between a manticore and a firecrab.

262. Muggles call this flightless bird the dodo.

263. Serves as a guardian for a tree whose wood is used for making wands.

264. Crab-like parasite commonly found in the fur and feathers of crups and augureys.

265. Elfish creature which uses its high-pitched cackle to lure children away from their guardians so it can eat them.

266. Small golden bird used in early games of Quidditch before the invention of the snitch.

267. Furry spherical creature which makes a lovely pet - it emits a humming sound when content.

268. Atlantic ocean fish which seeks out and destroys muggle fishing nets.

269. Small blue speckled bird - silent until it is about to die.

270. Five-legged beast also known as a hairy MacBoon.

The Weasleys (Hard)

271. What profession does Ron take up when he leaves Hogwarts?

272. Fred and George once turned Ron's teddy bear into what?

273. When Ron is about five years old his brothers, Fred and George, try and get him to perform what ritual?

274. After Percy graduated from Hogwarts he went to work for the Ministry of Magic in which department?

275. Name Ron's favourite Quidditch team.

276. Name the object Ron inherited from Dumbledore when he died.

277. What does the horcrux show Ron before he destroys it?

278. In *The Half Blood Prince,* Ron is poisoned by mead - but who is it intended for?

279. Ron is godfather to which of Harry's children?

280. Once Bill and Fleur were married they went on to have three children; what were their names?

The Malfoys (Hard)

281. What item does Lord Voldemort order Draco Malfoy to purchase from Borgin and Burkes?

282. Who is it intended for, and who ends up with it?

283. Just after Harry received his first broomstick at Hogwarts, Ron mocked Draco's. What make was it?

284. Who does Draco marry at the end of the Deathly Hallows?

285. ...and who is her older sister?

286. The two have one child together, what do they name it?

287. Which school would Draco have attended had it not been for his mother not wanting him so far away from home?

288. What is English translation of the motto written on the Malfoy crest?

289. What was the name of Lucius's father?

290. What were the names of Narcissa's parents?

Teachers and Their Subjects

Which subject do the following professors teach?

291. Professor Babbling

292. Professor Burbage

293. Professor Binns

294. Professor Flitwick

295. Professor Slughorn

296. Professor McGonagall

297. Professor Sprout

298. Madame Hooch

299. Professor Vector

300. Professor Trelawney

Spells (Hard) - Part 1

What would you say if you wanted to cast the following spells?

301. Clears a target's airway if it is blocked.

302. Creates a bandage and a splint.

303. Creates a duplicate of any object.

304. Makes a blindfold appear over a target's eyes.

305. Heals minor injuries.

306. Makes the target vanish.

307. Makes an enlarged object the correct size again.

308. Brings the target back to consciousness if they have been unconscious.

309. Conjures a serpent from the caster's wand.

310. Cleans a target object.

Hufflepuffs

311. Name Hufflepuff's Tri-wizard champion.

312. Which Hufflepuff student firmly held a belief that Sirius Black could transform into a flowering shrub?

313. When Harry first attends Hogwarts, which teacher is head of Hufflepuff house?

314. Which Hufflepuff student asks Harry if he really can produce a fully corporeal patronus?

315. Who had his name down for Eton school before finding out that he could attend Hogwarts?

316. Who gave Harry a public apology after wrongly believing he was responsible for petrifying students during the *Chamber of Secrets* saga?

317. What is the name of Hufflepuff's house ghost?

318. Who laughs at Harry's choice to teach the supposedly simple spell *expelliarmus* to Dumbledore's Army?

319. Who succeeds Cedric Diggory as Hufflepuff's seeker?

320. When she is commentating on the Quidditch match, whose name does Luna Lovegood forget, referring to him as 'Bibble or Buggins'?

Anagrams (Hard)

These are the names of Harry Potter characters, but the letters are jumbled up. Can you unscramble them?

321. Tabloid Bath Hags

322. Airbag Butchery

323. Nerdy Oven Slur

324. For Dicing Dry Frog

325. Cleared Our Flu

326. Label Extra Ringlets

327. Celery Novice

328. Yanks On Parsnip

329. Smug Fur Couriers

330. Lazy Harness Trail

Dumbledore and Family (Hard)

331. What is Albus Dumbledore's full name?

332. What is his Animagus form?

333. Before becoming headmaster at Hogwarts, Dumbledore taught which lesson?

334. Dumbledore is incredibly well known throughout the wizarding world, but the defeat of which wizard added to this fame?

335. When Dumbledore looks into the mirror of Erised, his deepest, most desperate desires are revealed to him, but what does he tell Harry he sees?

336. What are the names of Dumbledore's parents?

337. Where did the Dumbledore family live before they moved to Godric's Hollow?

338. Dumbledore's mother died in a terrible accident caused by whom?

339. Dumbledore is removed as chief warlock of the Wizengamot, but says he doesn't care as long as they don't eliminate him from what?

340. What are the 'few words' that Dumbledore says at the feast at the start of Harry's first year?

Pot Luck

341. What two other names is the elder wand known by?

342. True or False: the word 'muggle' is now listed in the Oxford English Dictionary.

343. Name the three unforgiveable curses.

344. Who founded the original Order of the Phoenix?

345. What is the name of the luck potion which Professor Slughorn brews?

346. In *The Half Blood Prince,* we're told the entrance to the headmaster's office is located on which floor?

347. ...and what statue conceals it?

348. Name the conductor of the Knight Bus?

349. Name Hagrid's brother.

350. With its streamlined, super-fine handle of ash and hand-numbered with its own registration number, just *how* fast are we told the Firebolt broomstick accelerates?

Who Plays (Hard)

In the films, who plays these characters?

351. Aunt Petunia Dursley

352. Dudley Dursley

353. Mr. Ollivander

354. Percy Weasley

355. Seamus Finnigan

356. Lee Jordan

357. Argus Filch

358. Moaning Myrtle

359. Professor Lupin

360. Viktor Krum

The Lovegoods

361. What is the name of the magazine that Xenophilius publishes?

362. When we are first introduced to Luna, what is her necklace made of?

363. How old was Luna when her mother died?

364. Near which village do the Lovegoods live?

365. In which Hogwarts house is Luna in?

366. Where did Luna and her father go on a holiday paid for by selling an interview with Harry to the *Daily Prophet*?

367. Who does Luna briefly replace as Quidditch commentator?

368. Name three creatures Luna believes in which other wizards generally don't.

369. What shape is the doorknocker of the Lovegoods' house?

370. Which animal head does Luna wear whilst watching Quidditch?

Who Said?

Name the character who said each of the following quotes:

371. "Alas, earwax!"

372. "You're a wizard, Harry."

373. "Why couldn't it be 'follow the butterflies'?"

374. "I shudder to think what the state of my in-tray would be if I was away from work for five days."

375. "You may not like him, Minister, but you can't deny: Dumbledore's got style."

376. "You are the most insensitive wart I have ever had the misfortune to meet."

377. "Reading? Hmm. I didn't know you could read."

378. "I can make bad things happen to people who are mean to me."

379. "You're the weak one. And you'll never know love, or friendship. And I feel sorry for you."

380. "But know this; the ones that love us never really leave us. And you can always find them in here."

Spells (Hard) - Part 2

What do these spells do?

381. Cave Inimicum

382. Repello Muggletum

383. Confringo

384. Deletrius

385. Orchideous

386. Langlock

387. Specialis Revelio

388. Mobiliarbus

389. Waddiwasi

390. Colloportus

Harry Potter (Hard)

391. In *The Chamber of Secrets*, Dobby visits Harry and Harry asks him to do something a wizard has never asked him to do before. What is it?

392. When Harry infiltrated the Ministry, who was he disguised as?

393. What extra subject did Harry take with Snape?

394. Which vault in Gringotts belongs to Harry?

395. When Ron is poisoned in The Half Blood Prince, what does Harry feed to him?

396. In *The Prisoner of Azkaban,* Harry is sat in the Leaky Cauldron watching a hag in a woollen balaclava who orders a plate of what?

397. In *The Philosopher's Stone,* Harry is sat in the great hall when he receives a long, thin parcel via screech owl - knocking which item of his food onto the floor?

398. Harry ends up having three children; what are their names?

399. What does Hermione use to cure Harry's bite from Nagini?

400. Over which city was the baby Harry Potter flying in Hagrid's motorbike when he fell asleep?

The Answers

Quidditch

1. Seven

2. Ten

3. 150

4. False - it is every FOUR years

5. Seven hundred

6. The final of the 1473 World cup

7. The Gimbi Giant-Slayers, The Patonga Proudsticks, The Sumbawanga Sunrays or the Tchamba Charmers.

8. Puddlemere United

9. Ireland and Bulgaria

10. Kennilworthy Whisp

Spells (Easy) - Part 1

11. Repairs broken or damaged objects.

12. A Summoning charm.

13. Causes an object to swell in size.

14. Disarms another wizard.

15. Used to fight a boggart.

16. Produces fire.

17. Creates a beam of light.

18. Magnifies the spellcaster's voice.

19. Causes the target to become confused.

20. Prevents nearby people from hearing a conversation.

Who Plays (Easy)

21. Daniel Radcliffe

22. Robbie Coltrane

23. Richard Griffiths

24. Bonnie Wright

25. Rupert Grint

26. Emma Watson

27. Tom Felton

28. John Cleese

29. Alan Rickman

30. Gary Oldman

Gryffindors

31. Lavender Brown

32. A milkman

33. Beater

34. A fox

35. Fred Weasley

36. Trevor

37. He had eaten poisonous doxy eggs as a bet.

38. Romilda Vane

39. Lee Jordan

40. Instructions that he would be doing his detention no matter how many party invitations he had received.

Harry Potter (Easy)

41. On his forehead

42. Lily and James

43. Slytherin

44. James

45. Eleventh

46. The Killing Curse (Avada Kedavra)

47. A Nimbus 2000

48. Vernon and Petunia Dursley

49. Ginny Weasley

50. A car crash

Hermione Granger (Easy)

51. Jean

52. They are dentists

53. Gryffindor

54. On the Hogwarts Express

55. A basilisk

56. Ron

57. A time-turner

58. Viktor Krum

59. The Sixth

60. Crookshanks

Hogwarts Staff (Easy)

61. Mrs Norris

62. Firenze

63. Skele-gro

64. Quirinus Quirrell

65. Professor Sinistra

66. The Half-Blood Prince, Snivellus, Snivelly, Sev or Slytherus Snape.

67. Hufflepuff

68. Dolores Umbridge

69. Charity Burbage

70. Professor Grubbly-Plank

Magical Creatures (Easy)

71. Acromantula

72. Centaur

73. Doxy

74. Flobberworm

75. Hippogriff

76. Kneazle

77. Leprechaun

78. Nargle

79. Phoenix

80. Thestral

Sirius Black

81. Padfoot

82. Thirteen

83. Bellatrix Lestrange

84. His cousin

85. He used his animagus form, as dementors were less able to detect animals.

86. The enchanted motorbike

87. 12 Grimmauld Place

88. Kreacher

89. Regulus

90. Snuffles

Spells (Easy) - Part 2

91. Avada Kedavra

92. Alohomora

93. Portus

94. Silencio

95. Expecto Patronum

96. Crucio

97. Stupefy

98. Prior Incantato

99. Obliviate

100. Morsmordre

The Weasleys (Easy)

101. Ronald Bilius Weasley

102. A spider

103. Bill, Charlie, Percy, Fred, George and Ginny

104. Fred

105. One of the Weasley's family owls

106. The Chamber of Secrets

107. Scabbers

108. Romania

109. A Werewolf

110. A Ford Anglia

Dumbledore and Family (Easy)

111. Fawkes

112. Gryffindor

113. Dragon's blood

114. Minister of Magic

115. Professor Snape

116. Ariana and Aberforth

117. His father, Percival

118. The Hog's Head Inn

119. Auburn

120. A pensieve

The Malfoys (Easy)

121. Vincent Crabbe and Gregory Goyle

122. A wounded unicorn

123. Moaning Myrtle

124. Charity Burbage

125. Unicorn hair

126. Lucius and Narcissa

127. True

128. Black

129. Hippogriff

130. A ferret

Who Plays (Medium) - Part 1

131. Maggie Smith

132. Ian Hart

133. Julie Walters

134. James & Oliver Phelps

135. Matthew Lewis

136. Jamie Waylett

137. Josh Herdman

138. Zoë Wanamaker

139. Jason Isaacs

140. Kenneth Branagh

Slytherins

141. He killed himself with the same knife he used to kill Helena Ravenclaw when he couldn't get her to return from Albania.

142. Millicent Bulstrode

143. Both are beaters.

144. Fiendfyre

145. Eight - he had to repeat his last year because he failed his exams.

146. Pansy Parkinson

147. Blaise Zabini

148. Theodore Nott

149. Graham Montague

150. Terence Higgs

Harry Potter (Medium)

151. The 31ˢᵗ of July

152. One year and three months

153. The Grim

154. Moaning Myrtle

155. Brazil

156. Basketball

157. St Brutus' Secure Centre for Incurably Criminal Boys

158. A Hungarian Horntail

159. Phoenix feather

160. The snitch from Harry's first ever game of Quidditch.

Patronuses

161. A Stag

162. A Jack Russell

163. A Horse

164. A Phoenix

165. A Lynx

166. A Hare

167. A Doe

168. A Cat

169. A Swan

170. A Goat

Hermione Granger
(Medium)

171. Hermione took the blame away from them after they were attacked by a troll.

172. The Society for the Promotion of Elfish Welfare

173. Winky - and by Bartemius Crouch.

174. Rose and Hugo

175. Ravenclaw

176. Because brainy students are usually sorted there!

177. Millicent Bulstrode

178. An Otter

179. The Tales of Beedle the Bard

180. The Protean charm

Anagrams (Medium)

181. Harry Potter

182. Sirius Black

183. Draco Malfoy

184. Luna Lovegood

185. Albus Dumbledore

186. Ron Weasley

187. Seamus Finney

188. Hermione Granger

189. Rubeus Hagrid

190. Neville Longbottom

Lord Voldemort

191. Marvolo

192. Death Eaters

193. Nagini

194. Wool's Orphanage

195. Little Hangleton

196. Elm

197. Gaunt

198. Borgin and Burkes

199. Dennis Bishop and Amy Benson

200. "Bone of the father, unknowingly given, you will renew your son. Flesh of the servant, willingly sacrificed, you will revive your master. Blood of the enemy, forcibly taken, you will resurrect your foe."

Spells (Medium)

201. Produces a jet of water from the caster's wand.

202. Ties the target up with ropes.

203. Makes the steps of a stairway flatten and form a slide.

204. Makes a target dance uncontrollably.

205. Cuts or rips an object.

206. Avis Oppugno

207. Homenum Revelio

208. Densaugeo

209. Rictusempra

210. Descendo

Ravenclaws

Hogwarts Staff (Medium)

221. Sitting in front of the staff-room fire

222. Professor Flitwick

223. Rolanda

224. Professor Kettleburn

225. Lilac

226. A Grindylow

227. Piertotum Locomotor

228. Budleigh Babberton

229. That they should be rounded up and tagged

230. Apollyon Pringle

Dobby

231. The Malfoys

232. He ironed them.

233. One Galleon

234. Aberforth Dumbledore's

235. In the gardens of Shell Cottage

236. A bludger

237. Winky

238. He used it to hide Winky in when she was drunk.

239. Harry's Wheezy

240. "Harry... Potter."

Who Plays (Medium) - Part 2

241. Hugh Mitchell

242. Mark Williams

243. Emma Thompson

244. Timothy Spall

245. David Tennant

246. Robert Pattinson

247. Katie Leung

248. Clemence Poesy

249. Ralph Fiennes

250. Bill Nighy

Hermione Granger (Hard)

251. Lavender Brown, Parvati Patil and Fay Dunbar - the fourth girl (who we're told is friends with Fay) is never named.

252. Lumos Solem

253. Needle

254. Freshly mowed grass and new parchment

255. Cormac McLaggen

256. A Thestral

257. Kingsley Shacklebolt

258. Mafalda Hopkirk

259. Dittany

260. Ten and three quarter inch vine wood wand with a dragon heartstring core

Magical Creatures (Hard)

261. Blast-Ended Skrewt

262. Diricawl

263. Bowtruckle

264. Chizpurfle

265. Erkling

266. Golden Snidget

267. Puffskein

268. Shrake

269. Jobberknoll

270. Quintaped

The Weasleys (Hard)

271. An auror

272. A spider

273. An unbreakable vow

274. The Department of International Magical Cooperation

275. Chudley Cannons

276. A deluminator

277. Harry and Hermione kissing

278. Dumbledore

279. James

280. Victoire, Dominique and Louis

The Malfoys (Hard)

281. An opal necklace

282. Dumbledore and Katy Bell

283. A Comet 260

284. Astoria Greengrass

285. Daphne Greengrass

286. Scorpius Hyperion Malfoy

287. Durmstrang

288. Purity will always conquer

289. Abraxas Malfoy

290. Cygnus and Druella

Teachers and Their Subjects

Spells (Hard) - Part 1

301. Anapneo

302. Ferula

303. Geminio

304. Obscuro

305. Episkey

306. Evanesco

307. Reducio

308. Rennervate

309. Serpensortia

310. Scourgify

Hufflepuffs

311. Cedric Diggory

312. Hannah Abbott

313. Professor Sprout

314. Susan Bones

315. Justin Finch-Fletchley

316. Ernie Macmillan

317. The Fat Friar

318. Zacharias Smith

319. Summerby - we're not told his first name.

320. Cadwallader - again, we don't know his first name!

Anagrams (Hard)

321. Bathilda Bagshot

322. Charity Burbage

323. Vernon Dursley

324. Godric Gryffindor

325. Fleur Delacour

326. Bellatrix Lestrange

327. Colin Creevey

328. Pansy Parkinson

329. Rufus Scrimgeour

330. Salazar Slytherin

Dumbledore and Family (Hard)

331. Albus Percival Wulfric Brian Dumbledore

332. A swan

333. Transfiguration

334. Gellert Grindelwald

335. Himself holding a pair of thick woolen socks.

336. Percival and Kendra

337. Mould-on-the-Wold

338. Ariana, his sister

339. Chocolate frog cards

340. Nitwit, blubber, oddment and tweak

Pot Luck

341. The Deathstick and the Wand of Destiny

342. True

343. Avada Kedavra, Crucio and Imperio

344. Albus Dumbledore

345. Felix Felicis

346. The 7th

347. A gargoyle

348. Stanley Shunpike

349. Grawp

350. 0-150mph in 10 seconds

Who Plays (Hard)

351. Fiona Shaw

352. Harry Melling

353. John Hurt

354. Chris Rankin

355. Devon Murray

356. Luke Youngblood

357. David Bradley

358. Shirley Henderson

359. David Thewlis

360. Stanislav Ianevski

The Lovegoods

361. The Quibbler

362. Butterbeer caps

363. Nine

364. Ottery St. Catchpole

365. Ravenclaw

366. Sweden

367. Zacharias Smith

368. Any of the following: moon frogs, blibbering humdingers, crumple-horned snorkacks, heliopaths, umgubular slashkilters, nargles, aquavirius maggots, wrackspurts, gulping plimpies and dabberblimps.

369. An eagle

370. A lion

Who Said?

371. Dumbledore

372. Hagrid

373. Ron

374. Percy Weasley

375. Kingsley Shacklebolt

376. Hermione

377. Draco

378. Tom Riddle

379. Harry

380. Sirius

Spells (Hard) - Part 2

381. Strengthens an enclosure from enemies.

382. Keeps Muggles away from wizarding places.

383. Makes the target explode into flames.

384. Removes evidence of previous spells cast by a wand.

385. Makes flowers appear out of the caster's wand.

386. Glues the victim's tongue to the roof of their mouth.

387. Makes an object reveal its magical properties.

388. Lifts a tree slightly off the ground allowing it to be moved.

389. Launches small objects through the air.

390. Magically locks a door.

Harry Potter (Hard)

391. Sit down

392. Albert Runcorn

393. Occlumency

394. Vault 687

395. A Bezoar

396. Raw liver

397. Bacon

398. James, Albus and Lily

399. Dittany

400. Bristol

Lightning Source UK Ltd.
Milton Keynes UK
UKOW01f1719090616

275934UK00024B/8/P